FOR ERIC,
WHO ALWAYS EATS HIS VEGETABLES
AND MAKES LIFE INFINITELY BETTER.

FIRST EDITION 2018.
LIBRARY OF CONGRESS CONTROL NUMBER 2018904743
ISBN 978-0-6929-8885-5
PRINTED IN THE UNITED STATES OF AMERICA
VISIT US AT WWW.SHANNONSCHNIBBE.COM

HAPPY READING! HAPPY EATING!

HERE'S SOME INFO YOU'LL BE NEEDING:

DEAR READER,
YOU MAY SEE SOME WORDS
THAT YOU DON'T RECOGNIZE,
SO TO HELP YOU, I'VE CREATED
A TINY LITTLE GUIDE:

*HANGRY: YOU'RE SO HUNGRY
YOU GET ANGRY AND YOU YELL.
*CARCINOGEN: A TOXIN THAT
MESSES WITH YOUR CELLS.
*LYCOPENE: A GOOD GUY THAT
FIGHTS CARCINOGENS.

ENJOY!
AND ONCE YOU'RE FINISHED,
PLEASE FEEL FREE TO READ AGAIN!

LOVE, S.S.

A IS FOR ASPARAGUS,
IT GROWS WELL IN THE SUN,
BUT PLAYS A SMELLY, FUNNY JOKE
WHEN YOU GO NUMBER ONE.

B STANDS FOR BRASSICA,
AND YOU SHOULD EAT BIG BUNCHES!
THEY SCRUB GUNK OFF YOUR INSIDES
LIKE A TEAM OF TINY SPONGES.

C STANDS FOR CARROTS,
AND YOU KNOW BECAUSE YOU'RE WISE,
THESE CRUNCHY CONES GROW UNDERGROUND
AND HELP PROTECT YOUR EYES.

D IS FOR DATE,
A WRINKLY, CHEWY FRUIT,
THEY'RE GREAT FOR CONSTIPATION,
BUT SOMETIMES MAKE YOU TOOT!

E STANDS FOR EGGPLANT,
IT'S A BERRY (WHICH IS WEIRD),
BUT IT'S GOOD FOR YOU AND FOUND IN FOOD
FROM VENICE TO TANGIER!

Fennel is a special herb,
it's great for a sick tummy,
and bonus points! It freshens breath,
if yours starts smelling funny.

G IS FOR GARLIC,
IT'S STRONGER THAN YOU'D THINK,
IT'S NATURE'S PERFECT MEDICINE,
(BUT IT CAN MAKE YOU STINK)!

HUCKLEBERRIES TASTE SO GOOD
AND HELP YOUR BLOOD TO FLOW,
BUT CAREFUL WHERE YOU PICK THEM,
FURRY FRIENDS MIGHT BE IN TOW!

I STANDS FOR IODINE,
IT KEEPS YOUR THYROID PUMPIN',
SO POUR A BIT OF TABLE SALT
BUT DON'T YOU GO A-DUMPIN'.

J STANDS FOR JELLYBEANS!
JUST KIDDING, NO, IT DOESN'T!
IT STANDS FOR YUMMY JACKFRUIT,
WHICH IS CHICKEN'S VEGAN COUSIN.

K STANDS FOR KALE,
THE **QUEEN OF GREENS**, THEY TELL US.
A SUPERFOOD SO STRONG AND GREAT,
THE OTHER GREENS GET JEALOUS!

L'S FOR LIMES AND LEMONS,
AND YOU SHOULD START YOUR DAY,
WITH A SQUEEZE OF THEM IN WATER
TO HELP KEEP COLDS AWAY!

M STANDS FOR MUSTARD GREENS,
GREAT FOR YOUR SKIN AND HAIR,
(THEY HEARD ABOUT KALE'S CLAIM TO FAME
AND DO NOT THINK IT'S FAIR).

N IS FOR A HAIRLESS PEACH,
CALLED A NECTARINE,
IT HELPS GET RID OF SNIFFLES
TO KEEP NOSTRILS SQUEAKY CLEAN!

O STANDS FOR OKRA,
IT ADDS FIBER TO YOUR DIET,
BUT CAN BE A LITTLE SLIMY,
SO SOME PEOPLE LIKE TO FRY IT.

POTATOES ARE GREAT ROASTED,
YOU CAN MASH THEM OR MAKE FRIES,
THEY'RE BURSTING WITH POTASSIUM
AND SPROUT FROM THEIR OWN EYES!

Q IS FOR THE YELLOW QUINCE,
A BRITISH, PEAR-LIKE FRUIT.
IT'S PACKED WITH ANTIOXIDANTS
TO HELP GIVE GERMS THE BOOT!

R STANDS FOR RADICCHIO
AND IT'S A HEAVY HITTER,
IT STRENGTHENS BOTH YOUR BONES AND BRAINS,
BUT TASTES A LITTLE BITTER.

S STANDS FOR SPINACH,
IT FEEDS MUSCLES SO YOU'RE STRONGER,
AND IT GIVES YOU ENERGY
SO YOU CAN PLAY FOR LONGER!

T IS FOR TOMATOES,
GREAT FOR YOUR EYES AND SKIN,
AND IF YOU EAT A LARGE AMOUNT
THEY BLOCK *CARCINOGENS!

U'S FOR UNDERWATER,
WHERE ALL THE SEAWEED GROWS,
IT'S A FULLY PERFECT PROTEIN
WHEN YOU'RE *HANGRY AND IT SHOWS!

V STANDS FOR VEGETABLES,
AND THESE ARE JUST A FEW,
BUT I BET YOU KNOW A GROWN-UP
WHO CAN THINK OF MORE FOR YOU!

WATERMELON'S WONDERFUL!
IT'S FUN TO SPIT THE SEEDS,
AND IT'S PACKED WITH *LYCOPENE
WHICH HELPS FIGHT OFF DISEASE!

(PRONOUNCED
SHO-KOH-LAH-TUHL)
XOCOLATL'S CHOCOLATE,
IT'S FRUIT! (AT LEAST, IN PART.)
BE SURE TO EAT THE DARK KIND
FOR A STRONG AND HEALTHY HEART!

YAMS ARE FULL OF FIBER,
WE DON'T GROW THEM IN THE STATES THOUGH,
IT'S LIKELY EVERY "YAM" YOU'VE HAD
HAS BEEN A SWEET POTATO.

Z IS FOR ZUCCHINI,
CALLED "COURGETTE" OVERSEAS.
IT HELPS TO KEEP DOWN SWELLING
AND HAS HIGH OMEGA 3'S!

OF COURSE, YOU KNOW YOUR ABC'S,
YOU'VE SUNG THAT FAMOUS SONG,
BUT NOW YOU KNOW WHAT FOOD TO EAT
TO KEEP YOU SMART AND STRONG!
SO GRAB AN APPLE!
BITE A PEAR!
OH NO! I LEFT THOSE OUT?!
ARE THERE MORE FRUITS AND VEGETABLES
THAT I FORGOT ABOUT?

LIST OF VERY IMPORTANT
FRUITS AND VEGGIES THAT GOT
LEFT OUT AND WE NEED TO MAKE
FEEL BETTER BY INCLUDING
THEM HERE:
1. APPLE
2. PEAR
3.
4.
5.
6.
7.
8.
9.
10.

Made in the USA
San Bernardino, CA
25 October 2018